THIS JOURNAL BELONGS TO:

_____

_____

_____

Trade Paperback ISBN 978-0-593-23177-7

Design by Danielle Deschenes
Photograph credits appear on page 176.

Published in the United States by WaterBrook, an imprint of Random House, a division of Penguin Random House.

INK & WILLOW ® and its colophon are registered trademarks of Penguin Random House LLC.

Printed in **United States of America**

2021—First Edition

10 9 8 7 6 5 4 3 2

SPECIAL SALES
Most Ink & Willow books are available at special quantity discounts when purchased in bulk by corporations, organizations, and special-interest groups. Custom imprinting or excerpting can also be done to fit special needs. For information, please e-mail specialmarketscms@penguinrandomhouse.com.

HOPE · FAITH · SUFFERING · JOY · SURRENDER · REST · GENEROSITY · LOVE

40
DAYS OF
INTENTIONAL
LIVING

A CHALLENGE TO CULTIVATE FAITH

THROUGH DEVOTIONS, JOURNALING, AND PRAYER

Ink &
Willow

CONTENTS

INTRODUCTION

> I have come that they may have
> life, and have it to the full.

> —John 10:10

When we hear the promise of Jesus to bring us life "to the full," we might pause and, with the best of intentions, attempt to consider the magnitude of how incredible that reality is, only to be swept along a moment later by the demands and busyness of our everyday lives. After all, how is there really time to reflect on the deeper themes of faith and spiritual growth when a work deadline is looming, meals need to be prepped, or kids need to be shuffled from one extracurricular activity to the next?

Still, no matter our hectic schedules and unending to-do lists, there is an integral part of us that longs for a deeper connection to God and a more intentional approach toward developing our faith. In his sermon "The Weight of Glory," C. S. Lewis addresses a similarly innate longing by tying it to the German word *sehnsucht*, which he described as "the inconsolable longing in the heart for we know not what." And as we all know, longings—whatever their source—yearn to be filled.

If you resonate with this idea for *more* in your faith—more focus, more depth, more intentionality—then *40 Days of Intentional Living* is the perfect resource for you. With thoughtful reflections from a number of beloved authors of faith, along with inspirational quotes, practical action steps, and beautiful illustrations designed to set your mind and soul at rest, this forty-day devotional will help strengthen your spiritual growth as it guides you through eight key themes of the Christian faith. In addition to daily journal prompts, each theme also closes with a reflection page, which will offer encouragement for cultivating intentional faith practices that can be carried on past the completion of this book.

Lastly, the forty-day structure of this devotional makes it an ideal guide for Lent or Advent. However, whether you plan to use this devotional as a guide through those seasons or simply as an individual or group-study resource at any other time of the year, our prayer is that through the next forty days your faith will experience exponential growth and you will know the nearness of God and allow His promises to take root in your heart:

The LORD your God is *in your midst,*
a mighty one who will *save;*
he will *rejoice* over you with gladness;
he will *quiet you by his love;*
he will *exult* over you with loud singing.

—Zephaniah 3:17 (ESV, emphasis added)

HOW TO USE THIS DEVOTIONAL JOURNAL

PLAN This devotional is divided into eight themes with five topics each, for a total of forty days of material. With that structure in mind, follow the timeline that works best for you. You can tackle one devotion a day for forty days, focus on one theme each week for eight weeks, or come up with your own individual reading plan. You know your own schedule, so pick a habit that will stick!

READ Each devotion is composed of the following elements:
- *Scripture passage and devotional reading*
- *Quote or prayer for meditation*
- *Journal prompt*
- *Image for reflection*

To begin, read the day's Scripture passage in your Bible or on your mobile device, and then read the devotion. Take time to reflect on how the message is applicable to your own life as you read the designed quote or prayer.

Next, answer the Journal prompt in the space provided. Feel free to add a personal prayer or any other notes as needed.

PRACTICE In addition to the above elements, there is a section at the end of each theme to reflect on the topic as a whole. This page includes a few targeted questions as well as a related action step that will help you on your journey of cultivating an intentional faith lifestyle.

Even when you complete this devotional, you can build on these action steps by establishing daily, weekly, and monthly faith habits and keeping track of them in the My Intentional Life section at the back of this book.

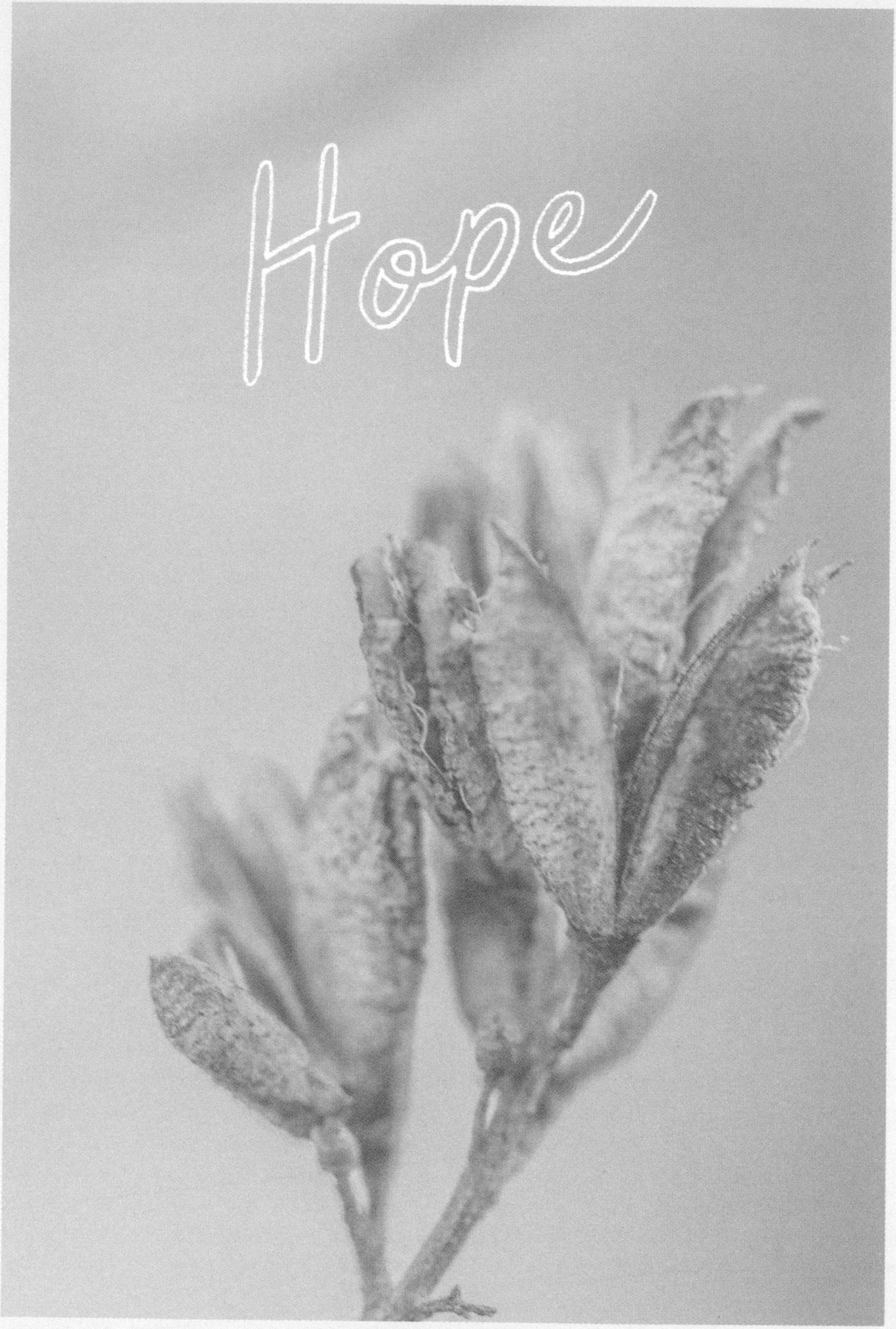
Hope

ll action movies have a familiar scene: The heroes have just lost a pivotal battle. Their resources, allies, and endurance are spent. At any moment, the villains will descend in full force and claim the final victory. As darkness—both literal and figurative—creeps in at the periphery, our champions are left to wonder if the fight was really ever worth it at all.

And there, in a moment that seems like an end, hope enters and ignites the spark of a new beginning. The way forward may no longer resemble the heroes' original path, but their final goal is more established than it ever was before. All at once, the presence of hope has done nothing and everything.

When defeat appears to be inevitable and the circumstances are darker and more hopeless than ever, in a beautiful twist, hope shines brightly. At the end of J.R.R. Tolkien's *The Two Towers*, the heroes are weary after a long battle and have no reason to believe the tide will ever turn back in their favor. It is in this hopelessness that Samwise Gamgee delivers one of the most powerful speeches in the Lord of the Rings trilogy: "it's only a passing thing, this shadow. Even the darkness must pass. A new day will come. And when the sun shines, it will shine out the clearer."

For the Jews living under the oppression of Rome, the new day they were hoping for revolved around the coming of the Messiah, whom they believed would free them from corruption and lead them to glorious triumph over the Roman Empire. Their hope turned out to be terribly misplaced, but the reality was actually much better than their expectation. For the Messiah did come, not as a conquering warrior but as a helpless baby. And not to build some temporary earthly kingdom, but one that would last forever, bringing light and life not just to the first-century Jews, but to all who call on His name.

How has hope carried you in the past? In what part of your life do you need hope right now?

Be strong and take heart,
all you who hope in the Lord.

—PSALM 31:24

WAITING

Read Psalm 27:13–14

There are times when you cannot understand why you cannot do what you want to do. When God brings the blank space, see that you do not fill it, but wait. The blank space may come in order to teach you what sanctification means, or it may come after sanctification to teach you what service means. Never run before God's guidance. If there is the slightest doubt, then He is not guiding. Whenever there is doubt—*don't* . . . Wait for God's time to bring it round and He will do it without any heartbreak or disappointment. When it is a question of the providential will of God, wait for God to move.

—from *My Utmost for His Highest* by Oswald Chambers
(Dodd, Mead & Company, 1935)

Waiting on the Lord isn't for the faint of heart. While we can know deep in our heart that His timing is the best, that doesn't make the waiting any easier. Look to His resurrection, be encouraged that nothing is wasted. Not even the time of waiting. Life often looks different than we would have imagined, but as we follow God, we can trust that His leading is best.

Write about a time of waiting and what you learned through it.

TEACH ME
AND SHOW ME
YOUR TRUTH
THIS SEASON.
MAY I USE WHAT
YOU'RE TEACHING ME
TO REACH OTHERS.

PATIENCE

Read Luke 2:25–38

When we hope for something, the timeline is usually very simple. We want whatever it is we're hoping for, and we want it now. Or better yet, yesterday. The idea of spending days, much less *years*, patiently hoping for something sounds nearly unbearable.

This is why a look at the Hebrew word for hope reveals a fascinating twist: the word *tikvah* (hope) contains the root *kavah*, which means "to wait." In other words, waiting is literally a central part of hoping.

Consider the wait times some of the heroes of our faith experienced. Abram and Sarai were told they would have a son, but it was eleven years before Ishmael was born, and *twenty-five* before Isaac was born. The Israelites wandered around in a desert for forty years before they were able to enter the Promised Land. The time between the end of Malachi and the beginning of Matthew is said to span *four hundred* years. And in the New Testament, when Jesus is presented at the temple, we encounter Anna and Simeon, who have been waiting for Israel's promised Savior for practically their whole lives.

Today we are also waiting—not for Jesus's initial coming, but for His return. The question is, how will we spend the time between?

In modern, first-world vernacular, when someone tells us to wait, we usually stop and sit still. But a second look at the above examples shows us a different picture. One that doesn't involve being stationary. Abram had to *leave* his homeland to fulfill God's promise. The Israelites were constantly on the move. Anna and Simeon spent their lives worshiping and praying in the temple. All of these are stories of forward momentum, even while the players in them waited.

Perhaps that is the real test of patience in hope. We keep waiting, and we keep moving forward.

What are you currently hoping or waiting for? How can you keep moving forward in patience as you wait on God's timing?

_____

_____

_____

_____

_____

_____

_____

_____

_____

_____

_____

_____

_____

_____

_____

Be joyful in hope, patient in affliction, faithful in prayer.

—ROMANS 12:12

ANTICIPATION

Read Genesis 22:1–14

God sees you and me in our pain and our brokenness. He sees you walking a difficult path when the sun goes down and your life is a far cry from that which you expected or dreamed up. He sees you, dear friend, when the ending of the story is not the one that you yearned for and your prayers seem unanswered and it all just feels like a bit of a mess. He wants to name these places The Lord Will Provide. In the places where you thought life might be easier, when you thought things might be different, when you thought *you* might be better, be more, God provides His Son, who meets you and provides grace for your gaps and light in your darkness.

His deep desire is for us—that we would know His love in these unexpected broken places and that we would know the true hope found only in His Son Jesus, the Lamb, who never, ever stops reaching out for us, who cups our pain in His nail-scarred palms and cradles our hearts close to His. He wants to be our reward.

It is a bold claim, to look up your mountain, to look out over the dry, cracked places and the barren places and the broken places, outcomes yet unknown, and call the place The Lord Will Provide, to believe that He will when we cannot yet see how. But perhaps that was the offering He was looking for in the first place. Just the believing. Just the hoping. Just the trusting. Just that our hearts would say, would truly know that "God will provide the lamb, my son." Because He did. And He does.

—from *Daring to Hope* by Katie Davis Majors (Multnomah, 2017)

Reflect on a specific time when God provided something in your life.
Return to this story whenever you need a reminder of His provision.

_____

_____

_____

_____

_____

_____

_____

_____

_____

_____

_____

_____

_____

_____

May I find
your promised
beauty in
my broken places.

GRACE

Read John 10:10

Cheap grace is grace without discipleship, grace without the cross, grace without Jesus Christ, living and incarnate. Costly grace is the treasure hidden in the field. Grace...is costly because it costs a man his life, and it is grace because it gives a man the only true life.

—from Cost of Discipleship by Dietrich Bonhoeffer (SCM Press, 2015)

Grace is a beautiful thing. It grants us the unmerited favor of God—His love—and He offers it to us with no strings attached. It's important for Christians to not lose sight of the price that was paid. Jesus willingly gave His life. Because of that, we can experience true life. Because of God's grace, we have hope.

What does true life look like? It's passing grace along to others, reaching out to a friend who needs encouragement, blessing a stranger, and living life fully in the purview of grace. When we live a true life, when we seek Him, when we don't live only for ourselves, we are able to see God work and move in amazing ways and spaces.

How can you live out grace today?

May I live a life that
reflects Your grace and
may I seek ways to share
it with others.

REFLECTIONS ON HOPE

1. What is one way your perspective on hope has shifted during your time journaling on this topic?

   _____

   _____

2. Identify an area in your life in which you could apply something you learned about hope.

   _____

   _____

3. Which aspect of hope (waiting, patience, anticipation, grace) are you committed to working on right now?

   _____

   _____

PRACTICE INTENTIONALITY

Every day is filled with small moments of waiting—waiting in line, at stoplights, for appointments, in drive-thrus, and so on. What is your first impulse in these moments? This week, practice using these moments as opportunities to pause and refocus your thoughts—either by recognizing things you are grateful for, releasing things that are causing you worry or stress, or looking forward to something with joyful hope.

BONUS Using the checklist page in the My Intentional Life section at the back of this book, make a list of things you are currently hoping for. Pray over the list, and then write one intentional action step you can take to keep moving forward in those areas.

Example: *I am hoping for deeper friendships:* invite someone out for coffee or tea.
I am hoping for a promotion: volunteer to take on an extra responsibility.
I am hoping for a new computer: make a revised budget plan.

I have quite a few definitions of faith that I've coined and collected over the years. Faith is climbing out on a limb, cutting it off, and watching the tree fall down. If doubt is putting your circumstances between you and God, faith is putting God between you and your circumstances. Faith is unlearning your fears until all that's left is the fear of God. Faith is the willingness to look foolish. And I've already mentioned it, but it's worth repeating: faith is taking the first step before God reveals the second step.

Let me give you one more.

Gratitude is thanking God *after* He does it.

Faith is thanking God *before* He does it.

Sometimes you need to stop praying for something and start praising God as if it has already happened. Isn't that what the Israelites did when they marched around Jericho? God didn't say, "I will deliver it into your hands"—future tense. He said, "I have delivered it"—present perfect tense. In other words, it had already been accomplished in the spiritual realm. All they had to do was circle Jericho until God delivered on His promise.

If you want to walk on water, you have to get out of the boat. That first step will feel awfully foolish. But that's how God turns the Sea of Galilee into a field of dreams.

If you want to experience the supernatural, you have to attempt something that is beyond your natural ability. If you want to experience God's miraculous provision, you have to attempt something that is beyond your resources. It might not add up, but God can make it multiply just as it did in a field of dreams filled with five thousand hungry souls two thousand years ago.

—from *Chase the Lion* by Mark Batterson (Multnomah, 2016)

Reflect on a time in your life when you acted in faith. Is there an area in your life right now where you could use some faith?

_____

_____

_____

_____

_____

_____

_____

_____

_____

_____

_____

_____

_____

_____

_____

_____

_____

_____

TO HAVE FAITH
IS TO HAVE
WINGS.

—J. M. BARRIE

PRAYER

Read Philippians 4:6

In the fall of 1999, I taught a Bible study course on the Psalms. It became clear to me that I was barely scratching the surface of what the Bible commanded and promised regarding prayer. Then came the dark weeks in New York after 9/11, when our whole city sank into a kind of corporate clinical depression, even as it rallied. For my family the shadow was intensified as my wife, Kathy, struggled with the effects of Crohn's disease. Finally, I was diagnosed with thyroid cancer.

At one point during all this, my wife urged me to do something with her we had never been able to muster the self-discipline to do regularly. She asked me to pray with her every night. *Every* night. She used an illustration that crystallized her feelings very well. As we remember it, she said something like this:

> Imagine you were diagnosed with such a lethal condition that the doctor told you that you would die within hours unless you took a particular medicine—a pill every night before going to sleep. Imagine that you were told that you could never miss it or you would die. Would you forget? Would you not get around to it some nights? No—it would be so crucial that you wouldn't forget, you would never miss. Well, if we don't pray together to God, we're not going to make it because of all we are facing. I'm certainly not. We *have* to pray, we can't let it just slip our minds.

—from *Prayer* by Timothy Keller (Dutton, 2014)

Beginning with a prayer of thanksgiving for what God has already done in your life, make your requests known to Him in this space, believing that He rewards those who honestly seek Him.

_____

_____

_____

_____

_____

_____

_____

_____

_____

_____

_____

_____

_____

_____

_____

_____

_____

_____

He who searches our hearts knows
the mind of the Spirit, because the
Spirit intercedes for God's people
in accordance with the will of God.

—ROMANS 8:27

THROUGH DOUBT (CIRCUMSTANCES)

Read Psalm 139:7–12

When life seems to bring nothing but a string of defeats and disappointments, we've got to have faith that something good is still in store for us. With this faith we can forge ahead and continue to put forth our best effort. Without it we give up and accept what comes our way. Our dreams turn to dust.

Are you troubled or confused? Faith is the answer. Are you burdened with grief or sorrow? Faith is the answer. Faith makes the difference between begging and praising, between crawling and leaping. No matter the problem—*faith is the answer!*

Indulgence may say, "Drink your way out." Science says, "Invent your way out." Industry says, "Work your way out." The military says, "Fight your way out." The world says, "Entertain your way out." Philosophy says, "Think your way out." But our Creator teaches us to "Pray your way out."

The world answers back to our faith. It trusts when we trust. It believes when we believe. It responds to our confidence. It says to the farmer, "Sow your seed." It says to the pilot, "Spread your wings." It says to the prospector, "Keep drilling." It says to the sailor, "Hoist your sail." It says to the infant, "Keep walking." It says to the newlyweds, "Walk together." It says to the downtrodden, "Lift your head up." It says to the surgeon, "Place your hand in mine." It says to the author, "Keep writing." It says to the Olymplan, "Keep training." It says to the achiever, "Keep believing!"

from *Daily Motivations for African-American Success*
by Dennis Kimbro (Random House, 1993)

What psalms or other Bible verses remind you to have faith in the goodness of God and His reign above all your circumstances and situations? How do you respond to the love God expresses in those verses?

_____

_____

_____

_____

_____

_____

_____

_____

_____

_____

_____

_____

_____

_____

_____

_____

Truly I tell you,
if you have faith as small
as a mustard seed,
you can say this to the mountain,
"MOVE FROM HERE TO THERE,"
and it will move.
Nothing will be impossible
for you.

—MATTHEW 17:20

Read Ephesians 1:4-5

Deborah was a powerful, wise, and strong leader. A judge and a prophetess, she was her community's spiritual and civil leader. She led secure in her authority and role, even in challenging circumstances.

The text notes that Deborah is a married woman, wife of Lappidoth (Judges 4:4). But the phrase wife of Lappidoth has more than one meaning. It also means "woman of torches" or "fiery woman." I think the words speak of both Deborah's marital status and her character as a woman on fire with a God-fueled passion and strong voice in her nation. Maybe like fellow prophet Jeremiah, she, too, lived with fire in her bones, with God's unstoppable words in her heart (see Jeremiah 20:9)....

It was Deborah who described God's military strategy for the battle (see Judges 4:6–7). And it was Deborah who gave the war cry to the gathered tribes of Israel. Deborah's voice empowered people to fight for freedom and receive their deliverance. Her voice sang their story when the battle was won.

Deborah didn't dial herself down in the presence of others. She didn't edit the acknowledgment of her contribution in a quest for (false) humility. She was bold, and in her victory song before an entire nation, she owned and named her place in the story. She didn't hide who she was or what she brought to the table. No, she owned it and talked—sang!— about who she was and what she had done.

—from *Ready to Rise* by Jo Saxton (WaterBrook, 2020)

Be Strong and Courageous

—JOSHUA 1:9

How have you been able to break through stereotypes because of your confidence in who God made you to be?

_____

_____

_____

_____

_____

_____

_____

_____

_____

_____

_____

_____

_____

_____

_____

_____

TRADITION

Read Matthew 6:1–2

The religious leaders of Jesus' day, the Pharisees, were the masters of legalism (tradition) in the church of that time. [They] talked about the life of faith, but they reduced it to mere religion, belief confined to words alone. They prized the use of the correct language but avoided the lifestyle of faith by every means possible. *They talked about faith but stripped it of life.*

Isn't that the problem we feel? Life can be filled with sermons but empty of life.

The "sermon" Jesus Himself is best known for, the Sermon on the Mount, isn't a sermon in any conventional sense. In fact, you could call it the antisermon, the speech that tells everyone that authenticity matters, that their message needs to be lived out in their lives.

I encourage you to read the Sermon on the Mount (Matthew 5–7). Notice how often the word hypocrite is used. Jesus is speaking directly to those whose words are not lived out in their actions. He calls people to act—live—differently from what was expected. Jesus consistently challenged the religious sermonizing of His world, calling people to go beyond words and live in a radically different and authentic way.

The problem of your life and mine is the disparity between the messages we proclaim and the lives we actually lead. And Jesus is telling us, just as He told the Pharisees, to talk a lot less and follow Him more. He's calling us to lift our heads from the noise of the words on the page and to look at Him, the living Word.

He's daring us to live lives consistent with who we are and what God calls us to do.

This is the adventure of being the message.

—from *Be the Message* by Kerry and Chris Shook (WaterBrook, 2014)

What Scripture rolls off your tongue but you struggle to put into action? Recount a time when it was easy to act upon that verse, and a time when your actions betrayed its principle. Share with God the tension you feel between knowing what to do and actually doing it.

Today, please help
me to truly embody
Your living Word.

1. What is one way your perspective on faith has shifted during your time journaling on this topic?

_____

_____

2. Identify an area in your life in which you could apply something you learned about faith.

_____

_____

3. Which aspect of faith (prayer, doubt, tradition) are you committed to working on right now?

_____

_____

PRACTICE INTENTIONALITY

Faith and prayer don't usually come easily. To maintain a strong faith and a healthy prayer life, we need to practice both consistently. This week, set aside at least ten to fifteen minutes each day for Bible reading and prayer. Track your progress below:

MON	TUE	WED	THU	FRI	SAT	SUN

BONUS Using the calendar in the My Intentional Life section at the back of this book, turn your ten-to-fifteen-minute Bible study time into a consistent habit. Pick a time that works for you (morning/lunch break/night) and then stick with it.

Suffering

Read Revelation 21:1–5

T here is nothing more practical for sufferers than to have hope. The erosion or loss of hope is what makes suffering unbearable. And here at the end of the Bible is the ultimate hope—a material world in which all suffering is gone—"every tear wiped from our eyes." This is a life-transforming, living hope.

Who was John writing to in the book of Revelation? He was writing to people who were suffering terrible things. Verse 4 shows you the list. He was writing to people who were experiencing death and mourning and crying and pain. This book was written near the end of the first century when we know the Roman emperor Domitian was conducting large-scale persecutions of Christians. Some had their homes taken away and plundered, while some were sent into the arena to be torn to pieces by wild beasts as the crowds watched. This is what the readers of this book were facing.

And what did John give them so they could face it all? John gave them the ultimate hope—a new heavens and a new earth that was coming. That is what he gave them to face it, and it is a simple fact of history that it worked. We know that the early Christians took their suffering with great poise and peace and they sang hymns...and they forgave the people who were killing them. And so the more they were killed, the more the Christian movement grew. Why? Because when people watched Christians dying like that, they said, "These people have got something." Well, do you know what they had? They had this. It is a living hope.

—from *Walking with God through Pain and Suffering*
by Timothy Keller (Dutton, 2013)

Think of a time in your life that was marked by suffering. How can you use that experience as a story of hope and encouragement for others?

_____

_____

_____

_____

_____

_____

_____

_____

_____

_____

_____

_____

_____

_____

_____

In order to realize the worth
of the anchor, we need to
feel the stress of the storm.

—CORRIE TEN BOOM

PAIN/LOSS

Read 2 Corinthians 4:17

Suffering will come; we owe it to God, ourselves, and those around us to prepare for it.

Live long enough and you *will* suffer. In this life, the only way to avoid suffering is to die.

Bethany Hamilton grew up surfing on the island of Kauai, Hawaii. At age five she chose to follow Jesus. When she was thirteen, a fourteen-foot tiger shark attacked her, severing one of her arms. Bethany returned to surfing one month later. A year later, despite her disability, she won her first national title.

Bethany says, "It was Jesus Christ who gave me peace when I got attacked by the shark.... And it was what God had taught me growing up that helped me overcome my fears...to get back into the water to keep surfing."

She continues, "My mom and I were praying before the shark attack that God would use me. Well, to me, 1 Timothy 1:12 kind of tells me that God considered me faithful enough to appoint me to his service. I just want to say that no matter who you are, God can use you even if you think you're not the kind of person that can be used. You might think: why would God use me? That's what I thought.... I was like thirteen and there God goes using me!"

Bethany and her parents had given careful thought to the God they served and his sovereign purposes. Obviously not every tragedy leads to winning a national title, but Bethany began where all of us can, by trusting God; in her case, with a support system of people having an eternal perspective. Hence, she was prepared to face suffering when it came, and to emerge stronger.

—from *If God Is Good* by Randy Alcorn (Multnomah, 2009)

How has God used your pain to draw you closer to Him? How has God used your pain to reach others?

_____

_____

_____

_____

_____

_____

_____

_____

_____

_____

_____

_____

_____

_____

GOD WHISPERS TO US
IN OUR PLEASURES,
SPEAKS IN OUR CONSCIENCE,
BUT SHOUTS
IN OUR PAINS:
IT IS _HIS_ MEGAPHONE
TO ROUSE A DEAF WORLD.

—FROM *THE PROBLEM OF PAIN* BY C. S. LEWIS

Read John 11:25–26

Easter is a day above all days.... The most righteous man that ever entered human history dying a most ignominious death. We look at him there and all that goes with goodness, all that goes with nobility, all that goes with that which is sublime, seems to be crushed now. And that was a dark moment.

But thank God the crucifixion was not the last act in that great and powerful drama. There is another act.... Good Friday may occupy the throne for a day, but ultimately it must give way to the triumphant beat of the drums of Easter.

—Martin Luther King Jr., "Questions That Easter Answers," sermon at Dexter
Avenue Baptist Church, April 21, 1957

In the midst of the darkness and pain in life, it can feel as if the burden will never pass. Or that our circumstances will never change. Imagine the depth of emotions the disciples felt at the foot of the cross. The man they left everything to follow had been beaten and died a sinner's death on that destined Friday. But it didn't remain Friday. And it doesn't today. No matter your circumstance, the darkness will not stay forever. It passes. A third day comes.

What hardship or struggle are you dealing with right now? Write out a prayer giving it to God and laying it at the foot of the cross.

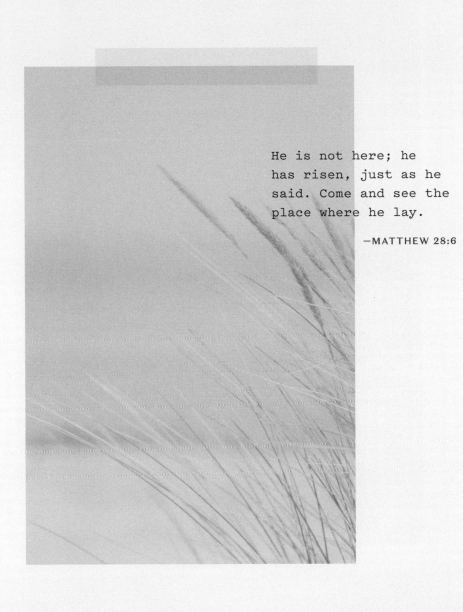

He is not here; he
has risen, just as he
said. Come and see the
place where he lay.

—MATTHEW 28:6

DARKNESS

Read Matthew 27:45–54; John 1:4–5

As the Heavens declare God's glory in the absence of other light, so God shows himself against the backdrop of evil and suffering—if only we are willing to look...and to discover that seeing him is worth even the cold darkness.

In the movie *Slumdog Millionaire,* the story's poverty, violence, crime, and child exploitation provide a backdrop for a young man's pure, unwavering love for a girl he met in the slums. The pair is tragically separated for years, and after they see each other briefly, she's taken from him again. Yet he never stops trying to find her.

Against impossible odds, the boy and girl finally reunite. He pulls back her *dupatta,* revealing a long, captor-inflicted scar that disfigures her face. As she looks down in shame, the young man, his eyes full of tears, holds up her face and kisses her scar. It's as if the scar itself is at last redeemed, somehow made beautiful.

That climactic, love-filled moment could not have happened without the story's disturbing setting of injustice, evil, suffering, and separation. He could not kiss her scar if she had no scar. Likewise, God could not wipe away all tears from every eye without the billions of tears shed because of the evil and suffering we've endured and inflicted (see Revelation 21:4).

If you put a diamond only in the light, you will see some of its wonders; but set it against something dark, then shine a light on it, and you will see magnificent beauty that otherwise would have remained invisible.

The gloomy backdrop of all human evil and suffering, including that of the cold, dark crucifixion itself, allows Jesus' grace and mercy to shine with dazzling brightness.

—from *90 Days of God's Goodness* by Randy Alcorn (Multnomah, 2011)

Reflect on a time when you experienced a greater sense of light after passing through a season of darkness. Consider whether you would take the idea of "light" for granted if you did not know "darkness." Record your thoughts below.

_____

_____

_____

_____

_____

_____

_____

_____

_____

_____

_____

_____

_____

_____

Maybe you
have to know
the darkness
before you can
appreciate the
light.

—MADELEINE L'ENGLE

PERSEVERANCE

Read James 1:2–4

The world is indeed full of peril, and in it there are many dark places; but still there is much that is fair, and though in all lands love is now mingled with grief, it grows perhaps the greater.

—from *The Fellowship of the Ring* by J.R.R. Tolkien
(Houghton Mifflin Harcourt, 1954)

Paul knew from firsthand experience how grief plays a role in each of our lives. From his personal experiences of persecution to what he saw in the early church, he understood how easily discouragement could come. But he also understood that more than grief and pain, there was light to be found in the darkness—God's love. In Paul's letter to the Colossians, he exhorts believers to be "strengthened with all power according to His glorious might so that you may have great endurance and patience, and giving joyful thanks to the Father, who has qualified you to share in the inheritance of his holy people in the kingdom of light" (Colossians 1:11–12).

Wherever you are, whether in fresh grief or working through old pain, be encouraged that love still grows and that the light of Jesus—God's gift to humankind—will always shine.

When was the last time you experienced grief? How did God help you through it? Write out some of His promises you held on to.

Blessed is the one who perseveres under trial because, having stood the test, that person will receive the crown of life that the Lord has promised to those who love him.

—JAMES 1:12

1. What is one way your perspective on suffering has shifted during your time journaling on this topic?

_____

_____

2. Identify an area in your life in which you could apply something you learned about suffering.

_____

_____

3. Which aspect of suffering (pain/loss, hardship/struggle, darkness, perseverance) are you committed to working on right now?

_____

_____

PRACTICE INTENTIONALITY

Walking through suffering, or comforting someone who is dealing with grief, can feel like an impossible situation. But we can always cling to the promise of the resurrection and find peace in the knowledge that God will never leave us.

This week, use the lined or bullet journal pages in the back of this book to write down Scripture verses, book or movie quotes, and inspirational sayings that bring you comfort. Reference the list whenever you're struggling with something, or share one of the verses or quotes with anyone who is having a hard time.

BONUS: Using the lined pages in the My Intentional Life section, write a letter to yourself that you can later pull out whenever you're walking through a season of suffering.

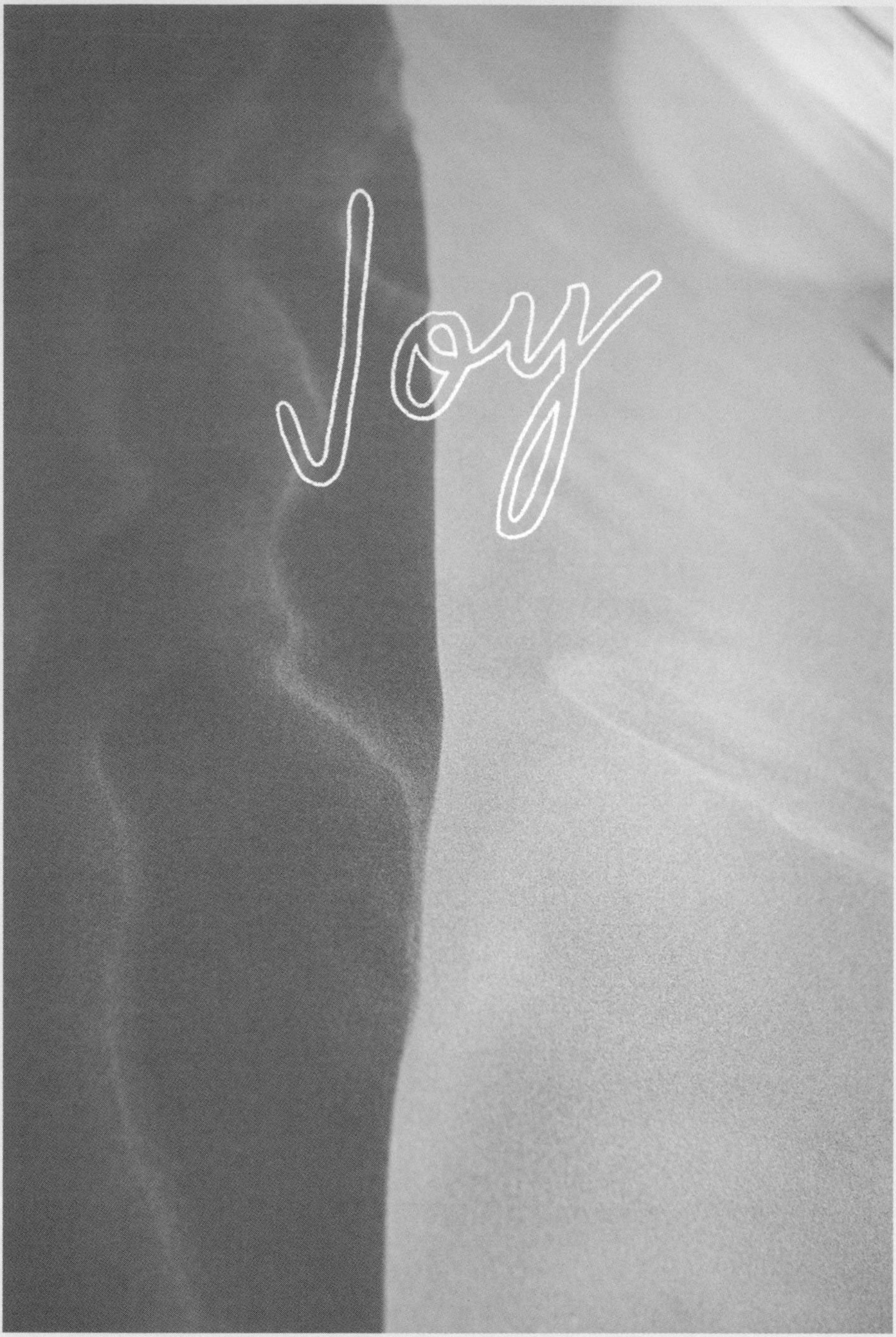
Joy

Read John 20:1–8; Luke 24:13–35

As we close the section on suffering, it seems only fitting that the theme to follow it should be joy, for when is joy more poignant than immediately after the dark?

J.R.R. Tolkien, the author of *The Lord of the Rings*, alluded to this idea when he used the Greek words ευ- (good) and καταστροφή (destruction) to coin the term *eucatastrophe*, or "the sudden happy turn in a story which pierces you with a joy that brings tears."[1] In other words, if a catastrophe is the worst unexpected thing that could ever happen, a eucatastrophe is the best.

Tolkien went on to say that "catastrophically" happy outcomes are so striking because they offer us a "sudden glimpse of Truth...that this is indeed how things really do work in the Great World for which our nature is made."[2] After all, when God created the earth, he said it was good. Thus, from the beginning, it is clear that God wanted us to know and enjoy good things. When we do, it is like a preview of the coming kingdom, when all will be joy.

Perhaps that is why happy endings in films, plays, or books often move us to tears. In those moments of breathtaking beauty, surprising wonder, and perfect inspiration, we are witnessing a glimpse of the way things should be—a fulfillment of the longing inherent in Creation (Romans 8:18–25).

These small moments of eucatastrophe, which cause our breath to catch and our hearts to lift, all point back to the original and best eucatastrophe—when against all odds and human expectations, Jesus defeated death, proving once and for all that it has no final victory over life. It is in that miraculous event where we find the source of all joy.

---

1   *Letter 89* from *The Letters of J.R.R. Tolkien* (Houghton Mifflin Harcourt, 1981)

2   Tolkien, *Letter 89*

What are the mental pictures that come to your mind when you hear the word *joy*?

Rejoice in the Lord
always. I will say
it again: Rejoice!

—PHILIPPIANS 4:4

HAPPINESS

Read Psalm 1:1–3

God made us: invented us as a man invents an engine. A car is made to run on petrol, and it would not run properly on anything else. Now God designed the human machine to run on himself. He Himself is the fuel our spirits were designed to burn, or the food our spirits were designed to feed on. There is no other. That is why it is just no good asking God to make us happy in our own way without bothering about religion. God cannot give us a happiness and peace apart from Himself, because it is not there. There is no such thing.

—from *Mere Christianity* by C. S. Lewis (Geoffrey Bles, 1952)

In one of his psalms, David wrote how only when we delight in the Lord can we attain the desires of our heart (Psalm 37:4). While we often assume that means if we pray hard enough and read our Bible every day, then we will get what we want, whether that be in relationships, career, finances, and so on. However, as we seek Him more through prayer and Scripture, our longings shift. They no longer focus on the things of this world, but our hearts become attuned to God's heart and we learn where true happiness comes from: God alone.

How have you found your happiness in God? Write out some verses about God and happiness.

_____

_____

_____

_____

_____

_____

_____

_____

_____

_____

_____

_____

_____

_____

_____

_____

Take delight
in the LORD,
and he will
give you
the desires
of your heart.

—PSALM 37:4

PRAISE

Read Isaiah 25:1

It's the potent combination of these two kinds of praise—praising Him for who He is and what He has done—that cause worship to always be an option for us, no matter what.

When we can't tell what God is up to, and we can't see Him working in our circumstances, we can still praise Him simply for who we know Him to be. Even if our circumstances don't appear to affirm it, God is still everything He says He is. So, no matter what life sends our way, we focus our attention on Him. He's still God in the midst of joy and tragedy.

In that same way, we can always praise Him for what He has done, though at times we feel we can't quite sense that He is near.

Our lives are filled with gifts from God, little miracles. Flowers every spring. The trees that line the road we take to work. The car (new or not so new) that gets us there. A chance to laugh. Eyes to see. A place to sleep. His faithfulness in days gone by. All of these should keep us worshiping moment by moment. Let's face it, gratitude for the gift of breath alone should keep us praising for quite some time!

We praise God for who He is.

We honor Him for all He has done.

Even if God never does another thing for us, should we cease to worship? Of course not—not when we remember all that He's already done through the gift of His Son.

—from *The Air I Breathe* by Louie Giglio (Multnomah, 2003)

Take time today to write out why God is praiseworthy and all that you are thankful for.

Lord, I praise you for
who you are. I praise
you for the beautiful
gifts in my life. Thank
you Lord for all you
have given me!

SALVATION

Read Romans 5:6–11

Many people in our day are searching for joy through material possessions, fame, success, family, work, rest, spiritual experiences, or a variety of other earthly circumstances. In salvation, God gives us a joy that rests on something eternal, something stronger and more secure than anything on earth. Our joy rests in Jesus: His perfect life, His sacrificial death, His miraculous resurrection.

Once we believe in Jesus, we become children of God. We're rescued from our old way of life and brought into a new spiritual family. Even though we've made mistakes and even though we continue to struggle with sin, if we are in Christ, nothing can separate us from God's love. And if we are loved by an eternal God, we have an eternal source of joy available to us.

In Luke's gospel, we see Jesus emphasizing this truth. The disciples returned to Jesus rejoicing that God was working in and through them as they ministered to others. However, even when they were filled with enthusiasm, Jesus pointed them to a different source for joy: "Do not rejoice that the spirits submit to you, but rejoice that your names are written in heaven" (Luke 10:20).

Jesus faithfully reminded His followers that the basis of their joy was not their ministry success but the fact that God had rescued and redeemed them. Salvation is the greatest gift we can ever receive. Our rescue is the source of abundant joy.

—from *In All Things* by Melissa B. Kruger (Multnomah, 2018)

THE JOY
OF THE LORD
IS YOUR
STRENGTH.

—NEHEMIAH 8:10

How do you think the attitude of believers would change if they truly recognized salvation as the source of their joy? How will you let it change yours?

_____

_____

_____

_____

_____

_____

_____

_____

_____

_____

_____

_____

_____

_____

OBEDIENCE

Read Psalm 16

Christian Hedonism is not new.

So if Christian Hedonism is old-fashioned, why is it so controversial? One reason is that it insists that joy is not just the spin-off of obedience to God, but *part of* obedience. It seems as though people are willing to let joy be a by-product of our relationship to God, but not an essential part of it. People are uncomfortable saying that we are duty-bound to pursue joy.

They say things like, "Don't pursue joy; pursue obedience." But Christian Hedonism responds, "That's like saying, 'Don't eat apples; eat fruit.'" Because joy *is* an act of obedience. We are *commanded* to rejoice in God. If obedience is doing what God commands, then joy is not merely the spin-off of obedience, it *is* obedience.

The Bible tells us over and over to pursue joy: "Be glad in the Lord and rejoice, you righteous ones; and shout for joy, all you who are upright in heart" (Psalm 32:11, NASB). "Let the nations be glad and sing for joy" (Psalm 67:4, NASB). "Delight yourself in the Lord" (Psalm 37:4, NASB). "Rejoice that your names are recorded in heaven" (Luke 10:20, NASB). "Rejoice in the Lord always; again I will say, rejoice!" (Philippians 4:4, NASB).

The Bible does not teach that we should treat delight as a mere by-product of duty. C. S. Lewis got it right when he wrote to a friend, "It is a Christian duty, as you know, for everyone to be as happy as he can." Yes, that is risky and controversial. But it is strictly true. Maximum happiness, both qualitatively and quantitatively, is precisely what we are duty-bound to pursue.

—from *The Dangerous Duty of Delight* by John Piper (Multnomah, 2001)

In what ways has your obedience to God brought joy to your life?

I have told you this
so that my joy may be
in you and that your
joy may be complete.

—JOHN 15:11

1. What is one way your perspective on joy has shifted during
    your time journaling on this topic?

    _____

    _____

2. Identify an area in your life in which you could apply
    something you learned about joy.

    _____

    _____

3. Which aspect of joy (happiness, praise, salvation, obedience)
    are you committed to working on right now?

    _____

    _____

PRACTICE INTENTIONALITY

Each day is full of small joys. This week, make a list of the things or moments that bring you joy. Keep the list in a journal, in the back of this book, or on sticky notes that you can hang somewhere visible.

BONUS: 2 Corinthians 9:11 calls us to share with others the blessings God has given us. This week, as a bonus practice, review your list of things that bring you joy and choose two or three to share with someone else. Feel free to use one of the checklist pages in the My Intentional Life section.

Examples:

- Coffee in the morning—make coffee for someone else in your house or pick up an extra coffee in the drive thru for a colleague.
- Curling up with a book and a fluffy blanket—donate some books or an extra blanket to a local shelter.

Read John 14:16–17

**W**hen you and I receive Jesus into our hearts and lives, He comes into us in the person of the Holy Spirit. And because the Holy Spirit is a person, when He comes to indwell us, we have all the Holy Spirit we will ever have. In other words, the newest believer has as much of the Holy Spirit as the oldest believer has, because we don't get a person in pieces. Yet regrettably, He seems to get us in pieces. We surrender to Him our Sunday mornings when we are in church but not our Monday mornings when we go to the office. We surrender to Him our Wednesday nights when we go to Bible study but not our Saturday nights when we go out with our friends. We surrender to Him our family but not our business. Our entertainment but not our eating. Our ministry but not our marriage. Our past but not our future.

Think about it. Ask yourself whether it's worth the cost to withhold some area of life from the Holy Spirit. Because His power in your life is activated in direct proportion to the degree you surrender and fully rely on Him.

The Bible records that the Jesus followers of the early church experienced multiple fillings. But it is interesting to note that while they were described by others as being filled with the Holy Spirit, they did not make this claim about themselves. Perhaps the reason is that people who are filled with the Holy Spirit are so totally focused on Jesus that they lack any self-consciousness.

This gives me pause. I wonder...What do you and I need to do to make sure we have surrendered every part of our lives so we can be filled with the Spirit?

—from *Jesus in Me* by Anne Graham Lotz (Multnomah, 2019)

What parts of your life have you surrendered to God? What parts have you held back?

All to Jesus I surrender.
All to Him I freely give.

—ISRAEL HOUGHTON

FASTING

Read Matthew 6:16-18

It's time to get a new outlook on fasting. When practiced the right way, fasting is something everyone should enjoy. That's right . . . *enjoy!*

I know what you might be thinking . . . *Isn't fasting for emergencies or for the really holy people?* No, fasting is for every follower of Jesus! Let me explain.

Too many people I know fast with a strict mind-set that focuses on abstaining. The fasting I'm talking about here is different. Of course it involves abstaining from some foods, but the mind-set is completely different.

I know several people who, once they began to fast correctly with a New Testament mind-set, did not want to end their fast even after their twenty-one days. Fasting is one of the most powerful spiritual weapons believers can use, yet many Christians have never experienced it. There is a common misperception that fasting is for serious Christians or only for times of crisis. Some even think fasting is an Old Testament thing. This couldn't be further from the truth.

I can say this with total confidence: *There is a closeness to God that you simply will not experience from prayer or personal devotions alone. You must fast.* You get a greater revelation of God's Word when you fast that you simply cannot get any other way. Disconnecting from the distractions of the world through fasting, and connecting into the power and presence of God through prayer brings a supernatural freshness and newness to our souls.

—from *Awakening* by Stovall Weems (WaterBrook, 2010)

If you have fasted in the past, how has it drawn you closer to God? What is something you can fast from in this current season?

_____

_____

_____

_____

_____

_____

_____

_____

_____

_____

_____

_____

_____

_____

FASTING
HITS THE RESET
BUTTON OF YOUR SOUL.

—STOVALL WEEMS

DENIAL

Read Luke 9:23-26

James Truslow Adams, who is credited with coining the phrase "American dream" in 1931, spoke of it as "a dream . . . in which each man and each woman shall be able to attain to the fullest stature of which they are innately capable, and be recognized by others for what they are."

The dangerous assumption we unknowingly accept in the American dream is that our greatest asset is our own ability. The American dream prizes what people can accomplish when they believe in themselves and trust in themselves. . . . But the gospel has different priorities. The gospel beckons us to die to ourselves and to believe in God and to trust in his power. In the gospel, God confronts us with our utter inability to accomplish anything of value apart from him. This is what Jesus meant when he said, "I am the vine; you are the branches. If a man remains in me and I in him, he will bear much fruit; apart from me you can do nothing" (NIV84).

Even more important is the subtly fatal goal we will achieve when we pursue the American dream. As long as we achieve our desires in our own power, we will always attribute it to our own glory. . . . This, after all, is the goal of the American dream: to make much of ourselves. But here the gospel and the American dream are clearly and ultimately antithetical to each other. While the goal of the American dream is to make much of us, the goal of the gospel is to make much of God.

—from *Radical* by David Platt (Multnomah, 2010)

In what areas of your life do you need to deny your own goals and instead put your life in the hands of the Creator?

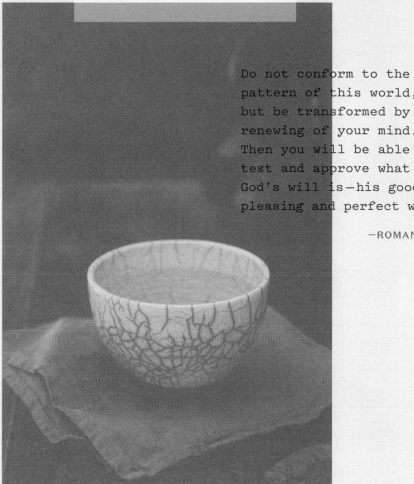

Do not conform to the
pattern of this world,
but be transformed by the
renewing of your mind.
Then you will be able to
test and approve what
God's will is—his good,
pleasing and perfect will.

—ROMANS 12:2

SELFLESSNESS

Read Isaiah 55:6

I renounced, for the love of Him, everything that was not He; and I began to live, as if there was none but He and I in the world. Sometimes I considered myself before Him, as a poor criminal at the feet of his judge; at other times, I beheld Him in my heart as my Father, as my God; I worshipped Him the oftenest that I could, keeping my mind in His Holy Presence, and recalling it as often as I found it wandering from him. I found no small trouble in this exercise, and yet I continued it, notwithstanding all the difficulties that I encountered, without troubling or disquieting myself when my mind had wandered involuntarily. I made this my business, as much all the day long as at the appointed times of prayer; for at all times, every hour, every minute, even in the height of my business, I drove away from my mind everything that was capable of interrupting my thought of God.

Such has been my common practice ever since I entered into religion; and though I have done it very imperfectly, yet I have found great advantages by it...when we are faithful to keep ourselves in His Holy Presence, and set Him always before us; this not only hinders our offending Him, and doing anything that may displease Him, at least willfully, but it also begets in us a holy freedom, and, if I may so speak, a familiarity with God, wherewith we ask, and that successfully, the graces we stand in need of. In fine, by often repeating these acts, they become habitual, and the Presence of God is rendered as it were natural to us.

—from *The Practice of the Presence of God* by Brother Lawrence (Nicolas Herman of Lorriane). Excerpt taken from *From the Library of C.S. Lewis,* compiled by James Stuart Bell (WaterBrook, 2004)

How has today's devotion refreshed your perspective on the theme of selflessness? How can you practice selflessness in your daily life?

MAY I GIVE THANKS
FOR <u>HIS</u> GREAT GOODNESS
TOWARD ME, WHICH I
CAN NEVER SUFFICIENTLY
MARVEL AT.

RESURRECTION

Read Matthew 14:22–33

When Jesus called Peter to come to him across the water, Peter, for one brief, glorious moment, remembered how and strode with ease across the lake. This is how we are meant to be, and then we forget, and we sink. But if we cry out for help (as Peter did) we will be pulled out of the water; we won't drown. And if we listen, we will hear; and if we look, we will see.

The impossible still happens to us, often during the work, sometimes when we are so tired that inadvertently we let down all the barriers we have built up. We lose our adult skepticism and become once again children who can walk down their grandmother's winding stairs without touching.

It is one of those impossibilities I believe in; and in believing, my own feet touch the surface of the lake, and I go to meet him, like Peter, walking on water.

But only if I die first, only if I am willing to die. I am mortal, flawed, trapped in my own skin, my own barely used brain, I do not understand this death, but I am learning to trust it. Only through this death can come the glory of resurrection; only through this death can come birth.

And I cannot do it myself. It is not easy to think of any kind of death as a gift, but it is prefigured for us in the mighty acts of Creation and Incarnation; in Crucifixion and Resurrection.

—from *Walking on Water* by Madeleine L'Engle (WaterBrook, 1998)

Describe a book or movie that represents the idea of resurrection for you.

_____

_____

_____

_____

_____

_____

_____

_____

_____

_____

_____

_____

_____

_____

_____

_____

Love is not power.
Love is giving
power away.

—MADELEINE L'ENGLE

1. What is one way your perspective on surrender has shifted during your time journaling on this topic?

   _____

   _____

2. Identify an area in your life in which you could apply something you learned about surrender.

   _____

   _____

3. Which aspect of surrender (fasting, denial, selflessness, resurrection) are you committed to working on right now?

   _____

   _____

PRACTICE INTENTIONALITY

One tangible way that believers practice surrender is through fasting. Although fasting often involves giving up food for a time, several other ways to observe the practice exist. You might give up chocolate, TV, gossiping, or social media use, but the important thing to remember is to choose a "fast" that will draw you deeper in your walk with God.

This week, search your habits or addictions and choose something to give up. Whatever you decide on, try to replace that thing with a healthy spiritual practice.

Example: *This week, I'm fasting from hitting the snooze button on my alarm. In its place, I will read a psalm or spend time in prayer.*

BONUS: Using the habit calendar at the back of this book, challenge yourself to extend your fast to two weeks or more.

Rest

Jesus had infinite power and potential. He personally embodied the most important calling and mission in history. He did so much in His lifetime that John would later say the world could not contain the books describing His works. Yet notice *when* He received His Father's approval: at the *beginning* of His ministry—before He even officially started His mission. Now, if the Father's acceptance of Jesus was based in something that preceded His accomplishments, what makes you think you could do anything to knock God's socks off or to obtain His acceptance through your accomplishments?

Many Christians spend a lifetime trying to achieve something that Jesus already achieved for them. God's acceptance isn't based on performance. It wasn't for Jesus. And because of what He did for you, it isn't for you either.

The acceptance He had, you have. The love He unconditionally received, you unconditionally receive.

Yes, Jesus was the Son of God. But through Him, you are a child of God with the same privileges. That includes the privilege of having God look at you and say, "I am well pleased."

When you realize that God is the only One who really has any lasting reward to give, He becomes the only One whose approval you desperately need. You can rest in the fact that you have it—in full measure—because the work of God's perfect Son, Jesus, secured your acceptance the moment you placed your faith in Him.

Before you ever win or lose, God has turned His face toward you. He has chosen you. And He is pleased.

—from *Crash the Chatterbox* by Steven Furtick (Multnomah, 2014)

Reread today's Bible passage from Matthew about Jesus's baptism. Journal on what the Holy Spirit is saying to you and pray through anything God may be teaching you through the passage. Rest in silence as you reflect on the truth that Jesus's work is finished and that God is rejoicing over you.

No matter what destructive
and damaging names you've
been called, they aren't
the ones that matter. The
ones that matter are Worthy,
Valuable, Chosen, and
Beloved. These names remind
you that you weren't, in
fact, a mistake but a person
who needed to live.

—ASHLEE EILAND, *HUMAN(KIND)*

SILENCE

Read Psalm 62:5

Friend, we were physically built for silence. God designed us this way, and science confirms that design. Secondary to the spiritual impact of time alone with God, according to the emerging field of neurotheology, quiet meditation quite literally changes our brains.

When we turn off the constant distractions and sit quietly before God, focusing intently on His Word and really meditating on it, a few things happen:

- Your brain will be physiologically altered. "Scientists have found that the brains of people who spend untold hours in prayer and meditation are different."

- Your imagination will be rewired. "Inappropriate thoughts can be combatted with positive thoughts, such as thinking of a new hobby, playing music, repeating an inspiring quote, or some other positive activity," wrote Sam Black from Covenant Eyes.

- The kind of brain waves present during relaxation increases, and anxiety and depression decrease. "Several studies have demonstrated that subjects who meditated for a short time showed increased alpha waves (the relaxed brain waves) and decreased anxiety and depression."

- Your brain stays younger longer. "A study from UCLA found that long-term meditators had better-preserved brains than non-meditators as they aged."

- You'll have fewer wandering thoughts. "One of the most interesting studies in the last few years, carried out at Yale University, found that mindfulness meditation decreases activity in the default mode network (DMN), the brain network responsible for mind-wandering and self-referential thoughts—a.k.a., 'monkey mind.'"

- Your perspective will eventually shift. "When we take time to listen to what God has to say to us," wrote Bible teacher Charles Stanley, "we will see how much He loves us and wants to help us through every situation in life. He gives us the confidence to live extraordinary lives in the power of His Spirit and grace."

—from *Get Out of Your Head* by Jennie Allen (WaterBrook, 2020)

Take time to write out things in which you want to hear from God. After you do, take time to be silent as you wait on Him to answer.

MAY I TAKE TIME TO BE SILENT.
TO SHUT OUT THE BUSY,
THE DISTRACTIONS, AND WHAT
I DON'T NEED. HELP ME TO BE
QUIET, SO THAT IN TURN,
I CAN HEAR YOU MORE.

SOLITUDE

Read Luke 6:12

Easy and light. Does [that] describe any aspect of your life? Is it a prevalent characteristic of the "leaders" you look up to? Does ease and lightness mark the lives of your spiritual fathers and mothers? The cultural ethos we've had burned into our brains since we were kids has been "Work hard, play hard." Work as hard as you can, and then you get your much-deserved rest. "Work for rest." That's what we're told to do. Most of us don't even suspect there could be another way. Is working for rest an idea for the lazy? Is it just an impractical fantasy?

These are tough questions that don't always have simple answers. However, I'm learning more and more that God doesn't want me to be in chaos. He wants me to rest. He wants me to have a deep unshakable joy in my soul. He wants me to really act like I'm accepted.

Jesus demonstrated this for us with astonishing humility. He was not afraid to acknowledge His unending need for the Father's presence. Time and again Jesus walked away from the swarming throngs of people and sought out desolate places where He could be with His Father. He obviously found something in the Father's presence that He wasn't able to access in any other way. He knew where His help came from.

If we are to follow Jesus, then we must follow Him in this regard as well. If Jesus needed time with His Father, how much more do we?

—from *Finding God's Life for My Will* by Mike Donehey (WaterBrook, 2019)

Whether you enjoy alone time or tend to avoid it at all costs, try sitting in a quiet space without distractions and jotting down the thoughts that come to mind.

Come to me, all you who are weary and burdened, and I will give you rest. Take my yoke upon you and learn from me, for I am gentle and humble in heart, and you will find rest for your souls.

—MATTHEW 11:28-29

PRESENCE

Read Ephesians 5:15–20

I'm just old enough to remember this thing from the late '90s we called "boredom."

There was a time when you'd be flying across the country, somewhere over, say, Minnesota, and you'd finish your book earlier than expected and just...stare out the window. With nothing to do.

Or you'd be waiting in line at your coffee shop of choice, five people ahead of you, and you'd have to just stand there. The extroverts in line would all strike up a conversation. We introverts would smile and nod, secretly thinking, *Why, dear God, is this total stranger talking to me?*

And while it's easy to sentimentalize something as inane as boredom, none of us, honestly, wants to go back to a predigital world.

But again, pros and cons. We now have access to infinity through our new cyborgesque selves, which is great, but we've also lost something crucial. All those little moments of boredom were potential portals to prayer. Little moments throughout our days to wake up to the reality of God all around us. To wake up to our own souls. To draw our minds' attention back to God; to come off the hurry drug and come home to awareness.

Now all those little moments are gone, swallowed up by the digital carnivore . . .

All this has profound implications for our apprenticeships to Jesus and our experiences of the life he has on offer. How so? Simple: this new normal of hurried digital distraction is robbing us of the ability to be *present.*

Present to God.

Present to other people.

Present to all that is good, beautiful, and true in our world.

Even present to our own souls.

—from *The Ruthless Elimination of Hurry* by John Mark Comer
(WaterBrook, 2019)

Write down some thoughts about how you can practice presence in your own life.

MAY I TAKE MOMENTS EACH DAY TO REFOCUS AND SEE WITH INTENTION THE PEOPLE AND PLACES AROUND ME.

PEACE

Read Colossians 3:15

The path of peace comes only when we're willing to walk into our own darkness and face our own shadows. We must face the very things that steal our peace from us whether they are born out of our fear or our doubts. The concept of peace is deeply rooted in the history that shaped the world and culture of Jesus's day. The Hebrew word for "peace" is *shalom*. The word *shalom* is layered, complex, and elegant in its nuances. At its most superficial level, *shalom* is basically used as a form of greeting. In many ways it can be compared with the English word *goodbye*, which is simply a part of our common language but is rooted in the phrase "God be with you."

Shalom is a greeting with deep implications. It is most commonly translated and understood to mean "peace," but the peace of shalom is rich in its textures. The word extends beyond meaning "peace" to meaning "harmony, wholeness, completeness, prosperity, welfare, and tranquillity." To experience shalom is to find wholeness. When we find peace, we are made whole. The ultimate goal of peace is that we not only are made whole within ourselves but also become part of the whole within all of creation. The very concept of *shalom* assumes that the original intention of God is for all things to be interconnected—that when there is peace, there is relationship and harmony between all things.

—from *The Way of the Warrior*
by Erwin Raphael McManus (WaterBrook, 2019)

How do you experience God's peace? Where? How can you do that today?

May I recognize
the moments of
shalom in my life
and understand that
by You alone I can
experience it.

1. What is one way your perspective on rest has shifted during your time journaling on this topic?

    _____

    _____

2. Identify an area in your life in which you could apply something you learned about rest.

    _____

    _____

3. Which aspect of rest (silence, solitude, presence, peace) are you committed to working on right now?

    _____

    _____

PRACTICE INTENTIONALITY

In our media-driven, attention-demanding culture, finding rest can feel impossible. But as we've seen from the life of Jesus, it can be done.

This week, whenever you have a "down" minute and find yourself reaching for your phone or the Netflix queue, resist the urge and do something truly restful instead. Take a power nap. Read an old-fashioned physical book. Go on a walk. Play an instrument. Have a face-to-face conversation with someone.

BONUS: Using the habit calendar in the My Intentional Life section at the back of this book, challenge yourself to go an entire day or even two each week without social media (barring work responsibilities). Track how many weeks you keep your goal.

Generosity

Read John 6:1–13

hat comes to mind when you think about hospitality? Maybe you start thinking about hosting dinner parties, inviting friends into your home, or searching the internet to download "company worthy" recipes that you'll spend all day making. Maybe even the thought of hosting stresses you out. But biblical hospitality is not about impressing, and it's not reserved for the gifted few.

Biblical hospitality is, literally, "love of strangers," and we are all called to practice it. Hospitality is about service to others, not about performance. Hospitality is not meant to show off our skills as a cook; it is about sharing the gift of God's ingredients with others. Hosting gives people space to be themselves and to connect in an authentic, deep way. Can our humble homes and meals really do that even if we aren't particularly gifted cooks? Yes. And hospitality is worth the effort.

There is something magical about welcoming people into our homes. Sharing our private living space with others invites intimacy with them and requires our vulnerability. Hosting means we keep our (figurative, but sometimes literal) dirty laundry out for others to see. Our guests see the real, live thing, and that's a little scary. This sharing of ourselves puts others at ease because whenever we see the imperfections of others, we all exhale a bit, knowing we aren't alone in our messes. Sharing our homes reveals our humanness without our saying a word. Being together in a home automatically invites authenticity and gives us all space to connect in deeper ways than if we only met up for coffee at Starbucks, where everything down to the coffeehouse-vibe music playlist is managed for the corporate image. Hospitality isn't about showing off polished perfection; it's about serving strangers to make them feel valued and treasured.

—from *Tasting Grace* by Melissa d'Arabian (WaterBrook, 2019)

When has someone's generosity impacted you more than they knew?

No one has ever
become poor
by giving.

—ANNE FRANK

TIME

Read Romans 12:9–13

Often we're inspired to love others by giving of ourselves—offering what we have to help them overcome their problems and enrich their lives. We offer our bodies as living sacrifices when we give of our time, our talent, and our treasure. If you want to experience the full adventure that your life is intended to be, then you have to be willing to take action and serve those in need with God's love.

The Bible has a lot to say about caring for the needs of the poor. "If a man shuts his ears to the cry of the poor, he too will cry out and not be answered" (Proverbs 21:13, NIV84). God holds us accountable for how we use our blessings to help the poor and hurting.

Our greatest gifts—time, talents, and treasures—are essential to this process of maturing and building a global legacy. If you want to sacrifice something that no one else can give, then give part of your time to someone else. No one controls this commodity but you. How you spend your time reveals what's planted most firmly in your heart.

—from *One Month to Live, 10th Anniversary Edition*
by Kerry and Chris Shook (WaterBrook, 2018)

Reflect on a time someone showed you love by taking time for you.
Describe how that experience affected you.

_____

_____

_____

_____

_____

_____

_____

_____

_____

_____

_____

_____

_____

_____

_____

_____

MAY I RECOGNIZE

THAT WHEN I AM GIVING

SOMEONE MY TIME,

I AM GIVING THEM MYSELF.

RESOURCES

Read 2 Corinthians 9:6–15

When God provides more money, we often think, *This is a blessing.* Yes, but it would be just as scriptural to say, "This is a test." Abundance isn't God's provision for me to live in luxury. God entrusts me with His money not to build my kingdom on Earth but to build His kingdom in Heaven.

The act of giving is a vivid reminder that it's all about God, not about us. It's saying we are not the point; He is the point. He does not exist for us; we exist for Him. God's money has a higher purpose than our affluence. Giving affirms Christ's lordship; it dethrones us and exalts Him.

As we learn to give, we draw closer to God. But no matter how far we move along in the grace of giving, Jesus Christ remains the matchless Giver: "For you know the grace of our Lord Jesus Christ, that though he was rich, yet for your sakes he became poor, so that you through his poverty might become rich" (2 Corinthians 8:9). "Rich" in this sense is not about finances, and this is not the health and wealth gospel; God gives to us in a thousand ways besides material prosperity. No matter how much we give, we can never outgive God.

—from *Seeing the Unseen, Expanded Edition*
by Randy Alcorn (Multnomah, 2017)

Write down some thoughts about how you can practice giving away the resources in your own life.

_____

_____

_____

_____

_____

_____

_____

_____

_____

_____

_____

_____

_____

_____

_____

_____

_____

_____

What you keep
is all you have.
What you give,
God multiplies.

—CRAIG GROESCHEL

TALENT

Read Romans 12:6–8

Talent or passion? Which is more important when it comes to professional success? You might be tempted to think it's talent, but an eleven-year study led by Dr. Daniel Heller would argue otherwise. The study surveyed 450 elite musical students and found that, over time, passion trumps talent. It was the students' passion for music that inspired greater risks and gave them the intrinsic motivation to persist in the face of adversity....

Life is too short not to love what you do, so do what you love. The key is finding the place where gifts and desires overlap. God-given gifts are what we're best at. God-ordained desires are what we're most passionate about. And the place where those gifts and desires overlap is the sweet spot.

The apostle Paul exhorted us to use our God-given gifts in the pursuit of God-ordained desires. And he identified three traits that should define us as Christ followers: generous, diligent, and cheerful. No matter what you do, these three adjectives ought to apply.

The word *generously* comes from the Greek word *haplotes*. It's going above and beyond the call of duty. It's the extra mile. The word *cheerfully* comes from *hilarotes*, which means whistling while we work. It's an A-game attitude. And the word *diligently* comes from the Greek word *spoude*. It's having an eye for excellence, attention to detail. It's showing care and conscientiousness in everything we do. It hints at continual improvement. But there is a nuance that is easily overlooked. Diligence means delighting in what we do. And when we do that, everything we do is transformed into an act of worship.

Diligence is doing what you do with an extra measure of excellence.

Diligence is doing what you do with an extra measure of love.

—from *Whisper* by Mark Batterson (Multnomah, 2017)

THE PLACE GOD CALLS YOU TO
IS THE PLACE WHERE YOUR
DEEP GLADNESS AND THE
WORLD'S DEEP HUNGER MEET.

—FREDERICK BUECHNER

How can you cultivate your talents and passions toward God's calling for you?

SELF

[One] step toward breaking the spirit of comparison is to respond to God's call on your life rather than living for the expectations of others. Ronald Rolheiser writes, "So much of our unhappiness comes from comparing our lives . . . to some idealized and non-Christian vision of things which falsely assures us that there is a heaven on earth. When that happens, and it does, our tensions begin to drive us mad, in this case to a cancerous restlessness."

We see this restlessness in Peter until he moves from fisherman to shepherd. And we see this same restlessness in our own lives. As a pastor I have seen people go to college and earn degrees in fields of study they care nothing about, all to keep their parents happy. I have seen others run from the call of God and become successful in business but miserable in their souls. And I have seen people discover tremendous freedom by finding the courage to respond to what God has called them to and put in their hearts, even though moving into their call was hard.

Are you burdened by someone else's call or expectations rather than God's? What whispers in your soul have you been silencing out of fear or pressure or expectation? What would happen if you amplified rather than silenced that call and embraced it with reckless abandon? Thomas Merton reminds us, "We are all called by God to share in His life and in His Kingdom. Each one of us is called to a special place in the Kingdom. If we find that place we will be happy. If we do not find it, we can never be completely happy. For each one of us, there is only one thing necessary: to fulfill our own destiny, according to God's will, to be what God wants us to be."

—from _The Burden Is Light_ by Jon Tyson (Multnomah, 2018)

What are some ways you can be generous with yourself this week?

Purpose calls us outside ourselves—
outside our imperfections and obsessions
and into the lives of others.

—JORDAN LEE DOOLEY

1. What is one way your perspective on generosity has shifted during your time journaling on this topic?

   _____

   _____

2. Identify an area in your life in which you could apply something you learned about generosity.

   _____

   _____

3. Which aspect of generosity (time, resources, talent, self) are you committed to working on right now?

   _____

   _____

PRACTICE INTENTIONALITY

Try performing intentional acts of generosity this week. They can be small, like sending someone a handwritten letter (time), paying for the order of the person behind you in the drive-thru line (resources), or baking cookies for the neighbors (time/resources/talent). Alternatively, you could commit to something larger, such as volunteering in a local organization or at your church (time/talent). Whatever it is, be mindful to respect the specific dreams, gifts, and calling God has given you (self)!

Time: Resources: Talent: Self:

BONUS: Using the habit calendar in the My Intentional Life section at the back of this book, choose one or two of the acts of generosity you performed this week and make them a daily or weekly habit.

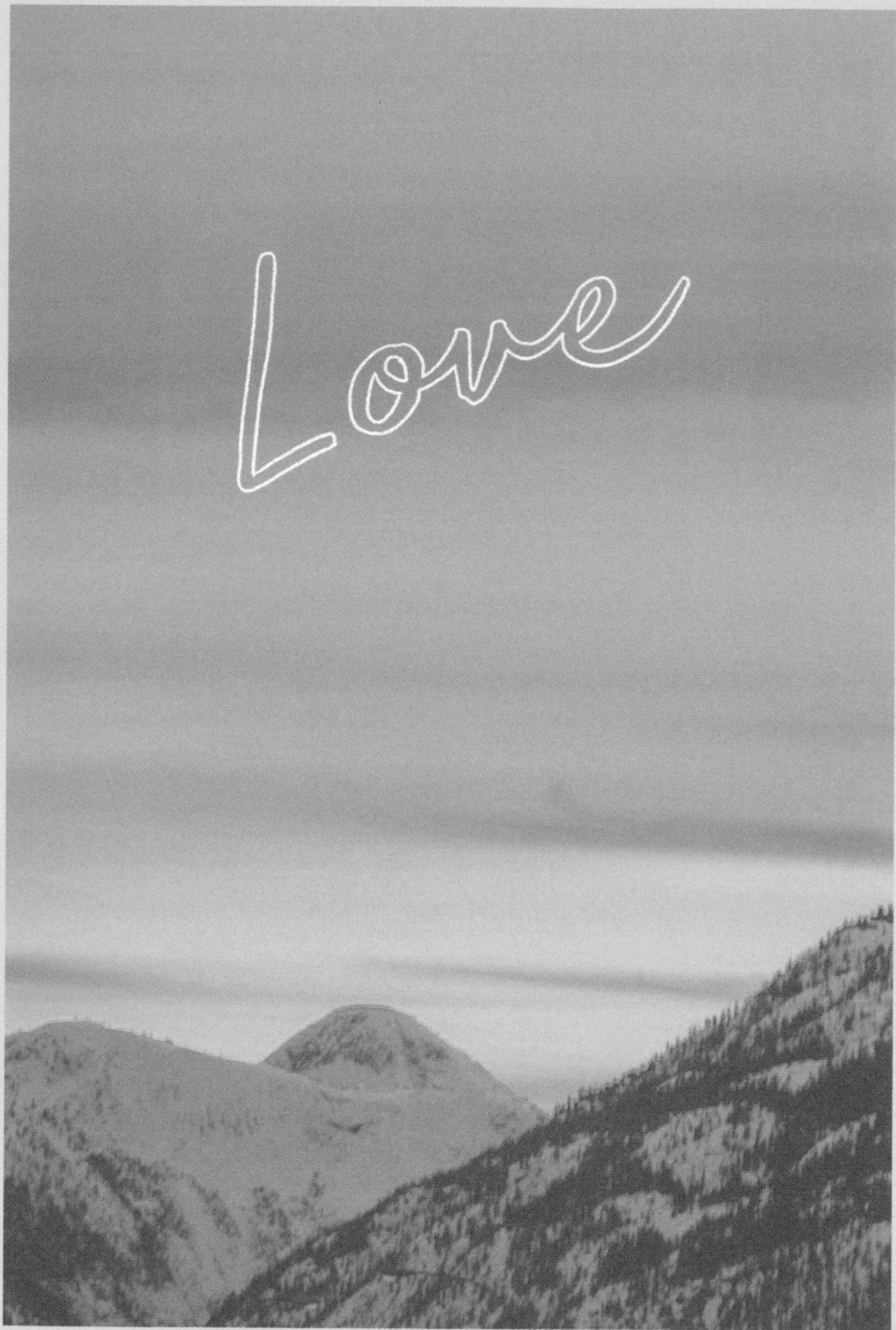
Love

Read John 3:16–17

I never kept a record, and my memory is somewhat faulty by this time, but I think I have fallen in love publicly thirty to forty times. The earliest time of which I have a clear recollection was in the first grade.... One of the significant things about these love affairs was that the girl, in the majority of the instances, never knew about it. I wanted her to know, but I didn't know how to say it. I wanted to express my romance, but I was fearful of rejection or scorn. And so I languished in a swamp of sentiment. And nothing ever came of it. My love never made anything happen.

You can't say that about God's love. His love does make something happen. The commonest misunderstanding that we have of love is that it is a feeling, a sentiment, a flutter in our stomachs, a tremor in our knees. But the love God has for the world is not a sugary sentiment. It is an effective action: God gave his only Son. And that action makes a connection between his love and our lives, between what he wants for us and what we need from him.

Jesus Christ is the action—a life lived in sacrifice and suffering, in truth and obedience, and in crucifixion and resurrection. God so loved the world that we might have eternal life. God's love and our eternal lives are connected by the Son. His love is made effective in our lives, not in the announcement sent out that he loves us but by the action of giving Jesus. Christ is born into our lives. This action makes God's love effective in us. It faces the evil and hostility of men, and by conquering that, it brings about our salvation.

—from *A Month of Sundays* by Eugene H. Peterson (WaterBrook, 2019)

What are some ways you have seen love in action recently? What are some ways you have been love in action recently?

_____

_____

_____

_____

_____

_____

_____

_____

_____

_____

_____

_____

_____

_____

If I speak in the tongues
of men or of angels, but
do not have love, I am
only a resounding gong or
a clanging cymbal. If I
have...a faith that can
move mountains, but do not
have love, I am nothing.
If I give all I possess
to the poor..., but do not
have love, I gain nothing.

—1 CORINTHIANS 13:1-3

SACRIFICIAL

Read Colossians 1:20

The action of blood is universal; it functions throughout the body, feeding the nerve tissues, the digestive organs, the bones, the muscles, and circulating throughout the whole system, having the power to restore any part of it. It is the same with love. Love is endowed with the power to redeem and heal throughout the past, present and future, and every part of the whole. The supreme manifestation of that love is the blood which Christ shed on the cross. This love enables us to believe in the forgiveness of past sins and the healing of past offences.

—from "Life in the Blood" by Toyohiko Kagawa in *Meditations on the Cross*,
transl. Helen F. Topping and Marion R. Draper.
(Willett, Clark & Company, 1935)

The most powerful stories in history, the ones people remember and pass down through the generations, are ones of sacrifice. From those of the Greatest Generation who served overseas and at home during World War II to individuals influencing the world today, they inspire us and change us through their sacrifices. And while they should, there is no greater atoning story than the one of Jesus on the cross. We are free because He died. His resurrection sealed our victory over death. Let us rejoice and live our life today with that truth.

Love is endowed with the power to redeem.

—TOYOHIKO KAGAWA

How has Christ's sacrifice changed your life? What are your favorite
verses on God's love?

VULNERABILITY

Read Ecclesiastes 4:9–12

To love at all is to be vulnerable. Love anything, and your heart will certainly be wrung and possibly broken. If you want to make sure of keeping it intact, you must give your heart to no one, not even to an animal. Wrap it carefully round with hobbies and little luxuries; avoid all entanglements; lock it up safe in the casket or coffin of your selfishness. But in that casket—safe, dark, motionless, airless—it will change. It will not be broken; it will become unbreakable, impenetrable, irredeemable.

—from *The Four Loves* by C. S. Lewis (Harcourt, Brace, 1960)

A great many things come from the high-tech, digital world, and each one has its pros and cons. Social media, for example, has made it easy to connect to people living a vast distance from us, but it's easy for those relationships to remain at the surface. These connections only require a light touch—a like here, a comment there—leaving us empty and feeling alone. Unchecked, this routine can quickly bleed into our face-to-face relationships. God created us to be in relationships and to have purpose though them. While opening your heart is risky and terrifying, the rewards are beyond measure. Fight the fear of getting hurt—it may or may not happen—and embrace the possibility of knowing and being known.

In what ways are you holding back love in your relationships (romantic, friendship, family, and so on)? What are ways you can push through and be more vulnerable?

_____

_____

_____

_____

_____

_____

_____

_____

_____

_____

_____

_____

_____

_____

_____

_____

_____

_____

There is no fear in love. But perfect love drives out fear.

—1 JOHN 4:18

THE LOVE OF JESUS

Read Romans 3:22–24

For there is power in the blood of Calvary to destroy sins more than can be counted even by one from the choir of heaven. Thou hast given me a hill-side spring, that washes clear and white, and I go as a sinner to its waters, bathing without hindrance in its crystal streams.

At the cross there is free forgiveness for the poor and meek ones, and ample blessings that last forever; The blood of the Lamb is like a great river of infinite grace with never any diminishing of its fullness as thirsty ones without number drink of it.

O Lord, for ever will thy free forgiveness live that was gained on the mount of blood; In the midst of a world of pain it is a subject for praise in every place, a song on earth, an anthem in heaven, its love and virtue knowing no end.... Though here my spiritual state is frail and poor, I shall go on singing Calvary's anthem.

—from *The Valley of Vision* by Arthur Bennett

(The Banner of Truth Trust, 1975)

How did you first come to know the love of Jesus? What was your understanding of His love for you then? How has your understanding changed, deepened?

Greater
love
has no one
than this:
to lay down
one's life for
one's friends.

—JOHN 15:13

AGAPE

Read Romans 5:6–8

There is a story of an old man who used to meditate early every morning under a big tree on the bank of the Ganges River. One morning, after he had finished his meditation, the old man opened his eyes and saw a scorpion floating helplessly in the water. As the scorpion was washed closer to the tree, the old man quickly stretched himself out on one of the long roots that branched out into the river and reached out to rescue the drowning creature. As soon as he touched it, the scorpion stung him. Instinctively the man withdrew his hand. A minute later, after he had regained his balance, he stretched himself out again on the roots to save the scorpion. This time the scorpion stung him so badly with its poisonous tail that his hand became swollen and bloody and his face contorted with pain.

At that moment, a passerby saw the old man stretched out on the roots struggling with the scorpion and shouted: "Hey, stupid old man, what's wrong with you? Only a fool would risk his life for the sake of an ugly, evil creature. Don't you know you could kill yourself trying to save that ungrateful scorpion?"

The old man turned his head. Looking into the stranger's eyes he said calmly, "My friend, just because it is the scorpion's nature to sting, that does not change my nature to save."

Sitting here at the typewriter in my study, I turn to the symbol of the crucified Christ on the wall to my left. And I hear Jesus praying for his murderers, "Father, forgive them. They do not know what they are doing."

—from *The Signature of Jesus* by Brennan Manning (WaterBrook, 1988)

What does the never-ending love of God mean to you?

THE LORD YOUR GOD IS WITH YOU,
THE MIGHTY WARRIOR WHO SAVES.
HE WILL TAKE GREAT DELIGHT IN YOU.
IN HIS LOVE HE WILL NO LONGER REBUKE YOU,
BUT WILL REJOICE OVER YOU WITH SINGING.

—ZEPHANIAH 3:17

1. What is one way your perspective on love has shifted during your time journaling on this topic?

_____

_____

2. Identify an area in your life in which you could apply something you learned about love.

_____

_____

3. Which aspect of love (sacrifice, vulnerability, Jesus's love, agape) are you committed to working on right now?

_____

_____

PRACTICE INTENTIONALITY

Love involves risk, invites vulnerability, and promises sacrifice. Yet love also brings change and healing. This week, identity someone in your life whom you could love better. Using the My Intentional Life section at the back of this book, write down three specific ways you can put your love into action.

BONUS: Loving those who love us back is easy, but loving without the hope of anything in return can be one of the hardest things we do. As a bonus, identify someone in your life who is difficult to love. Using the My Intentional Life section at the back of this book, write down three specific ways you can show that person love this week.

MY INTENTIONAL LIFE

Welcome to the practice-based portion of this book! In these pages, you will be able to put into action the themes, ideas, and goals outlined in the preceding devotions.

My Intentional Life is broken into four sections:

- Habit Calendar
- Checklists
- Lined pages
- Bullet journal

Though you will find some gentle guidance for how to use these sections in the Practice Intentionality step at the end of each theme, we hope that you will feel free to personalize and fill them in a way that best suits you. Whatever your preference, our prayer is that these pages will encourage and embolden you as you forge your own unique path to a more intentional life.

HABIT CALENDAR

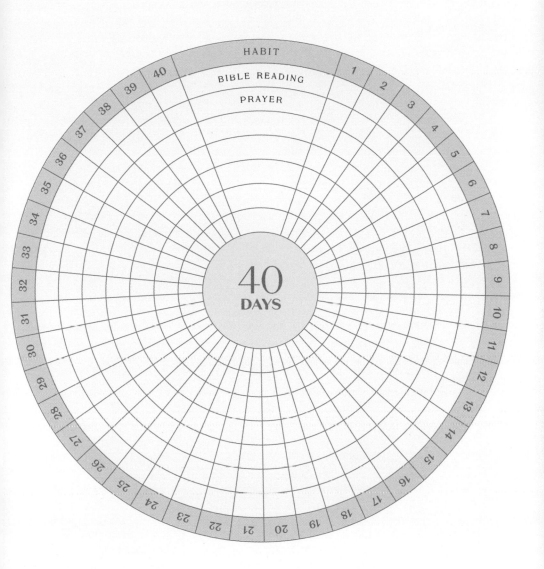

HABIT

BIBLE READING

PRAYER

40
DAYS

1 2 3 4 5 6 7 8 9 10 11 12 13 14 15 16 17 18 19 20 21 22 23 24 25 26 27 28 29 30 31 32 33 34 35 36 37 38 39 40

-
-
-
-
-
-
-
-
-
-
-
-
-
-
-
-
-
-
-
-
-

-
-
-
-
-
-
-
-
-
-
-
-
-
-
-
-
-
-
-
-